The Bald Eagle

by Lisa Trumbauer

Orlando   Boston   Dallas   Chicago   San Diego

Visit *The Learning Site!*

www.harcourtschool.com

Can you imagine seeing the wild turkey on our country's coins and bills? If Benjamin Franklin had had his way, you would!

In the late 1700s, the United States was a young country. It had won its independence from England. Americans wanted to choose a symbol for their new country. They wanted a national bird.

Benjamin Franklin thought the wild turkey should be the national bird. He believed the wild turkey was an honorable bird and a true native of America.

"He is a Bird of Courage," Franklin wrote. He would converse with others about his opinion, too.

Franklin did not want the bald eagle to be chosen. It was too fierce, he thought. Besides, other countries already had the eagle as their national bird.

Some members of Congress thought the bald eagle should be the nation's symbol. Like their new country, the bald eagle was free. It flew wherever it wanted to go. It was brave and strong.

There were other kinds of eagles, but the bald eagle lived on the continent of North America. It, too, was a true American bird.

Congress and Franklin never did agree about it. Congress eventually won. On June 20, 1782, they voted to make the bald eagle the national bird of the United States.

The bald eagle is on the country's Great Seal. The Great Seal is the official stamp of the United States government. The seal is a flat circle with two sides like a coin. It is used to stamp papers to identify them as being from the United States. Letters from the President often bear the Great Seal.

On the Great Seal, the bald eagle is shown holding thirteen arrows in one foot. The arrows are a symbol of power. In the other foot the eagle holds a branch from an olive tree. The olive branch is a symbol of peace.

The bald eagle is not bald. Its entire head and neck are covered with white feathers. Its tail also has white feathers. The feathers on the rest of its body are dark brown.

The bald eagle is not born with white feathers. A young bald eagle is all brown. When it is nearly five years of age, the eagle's head, neck, and tail feathers become white.

The bald eagle is a bird of prey. That means it hunts other animals for food. Bald eagles usually eat fish. They swoop down to catch them in their claws. They also eat other birds and mammals.

As the eagle flies high in the sky, its sharp eyes see prey far below on the ground. The eagle has long talons that help it catch and hold its prey. It uses its strong yellow beak to tear the prey into pieces it can eat.

The bald eagle is an excellent flyer. A bald eagle soaring across the sky is an amazing sight. Its powerful wings spread out close to eight feet.

The bald eagle can fly very fast. Flying level, it can reach speeds of 60 miles per hour. When it dives for fish or other prey, watch out! Then the eagle can fly up to 100 miles per hour! After it grabs its catch in its talons, the bald eagle often heads homeward.

A bald eagle's nest is called an *aerie*. It usually sits high atop a tree or cliff.

A male and a female build their nest together. Bald eagles mate for life. The nest they build will be their home for many years. They usually build the nest near a body of water so food will be easily available.

The pair of eagles constantly add to their nest, making it bigger. Their nest can be huge. It can be as big as 8 feet across and 10 feet deep!

The aerie is where the baby eagles are born. Baby eagles are called *eaglets*. In early spring, the female eagle lays one or two eggs. Then she sits on the eggs for about 40 days, or until the eaglets are ready to hatch.

An eaglet will start to chip away at its shell with a special egg tooth. An eaglet is born with its eyes open. It is not very strong, and it has gray down instead of brown feathers. After four to five weeks, the brown feathers appear. After about 10 weeks, the eaglet grows its flight feathers.

Being our nation's symbol did not make everyone like the bald eagles. Farmers once believed bald eagles killed their chickens for food. Some people hunted bald eagles for sport. As more homes and towns were built, people cut down trees where bald eagles lived.

Scientists believe that the bald eagle population once numbered 75,000. As the years passed, there were fewer and fewer of them. In 1967, the bald eagle became an endangered species. By 1971, only 2,500 bald eagles were still alive. Some people feared our national symbol would become extinct.

People were not only hunting bald eagles and taking away their habitat. They were harming eagles in another way. Some years ago, farmers used to spray a chemical called DDT on their crops. They used the DDT to kill insects that ate the crops. When it rained, the chemical would run into rivers. The DDT polluted the rivers. The fish living in the rivers now had DDT inside them.

The eagles would eat the poisoned fish. They didn't die from eating the fish, but when they laid eggs, the shells were very fragile. They often broke. This prevented more eaglets from being born.

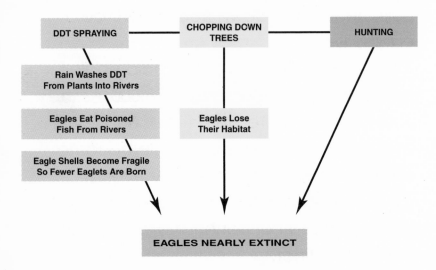

Congress again spoke up for the bald eagle. In 1940, Congress made it a crime to kill the national bird or take its eggs. Then, in 1972, the use of DDT was banned. Farmers were forbidden to spray the chemical on their crops.

The numbers of bald eagles slowly rose again. In 1995, the bald eagle came off the endangered species list.

Today, bald eagles are thriving once again. Animal experts think that more than 100,000 now live in North America, mostly in Alaska and Canada.

Bald eagles can sometimes be spotted in the wild around bodies of water. They range from as far north as Alaska to as far south as Florida.

However, you can see a bald eagle any time just by looking at a dollar bill! You can also see bald eagles on coins, such as the quarter, half dollar, and silver dollar. Once in a while, the United States Mint issues a special gold coin. It is called an "eagle." Why? Because the bald eagle is on it!

Eagles appear on other things, too. The U.S. Postal Service has issued more than two dozen stamps with eagles. Many businesses use eagles as their symbol. At the top of a flagpole with a United States flag, you might see an eagle with its feet around a golden sphere.

People like to be connected with the powerful, noble bald eagle. The highest rank in the Boy Scouts is the Eagle Scout. A football team named itself the Eagles. An eagle even played a part in the 2000 World Series. A beautiful bald eagle flew down to the middle of Yankee Stadium in New York City. Everyone cheered.

The eagle was highly honored on July 20, 1969. U.S. astronauts landed on the moon. The ship that brought the astronauts to the moon's surface was named the *Eagle*. As it touched down, astronaut Neil Armstrong said, "The *Eagle* has landed."

The moon landing was a great achievement, not only of science but also of courage and freedom.

The eagle now connected the United States to the whole universe. Not bad for a bird that once had to compete with the turkey!